Love Created Us

Living a Life That's Holy

Dan

Love Created Us
Living a Life That's Holy

ISBN: 978-1- 7356932-6-2
ISBN: 1-7356932-6-X
Library of Congress Control Number: 2021914504

Front Cover Photograph *Sunrise Gift* copyrighted by Sara Niccolls,
used with permission
Cover and text design by Helfried Zrzavy

Sacred Life Publishers™
SacredLife.org

Printed in the United States of America

From a Reader

Daniel Free is an open vessel into which the Word of God is being poured. He is patient and kind, and does not rush through life. His poetry and prose come from his willingness to be still and listen with a pure heart . . . a reminder for us to pause and absorb the healing balm we all so dearly need. Daniel scribes, "my soul is free," and this was clearly evident as I read this wonderfully gentle and reassuring book.

~ Joann Sjolander,
Co-author of the *One With God* book series

Contents

Foreword

I first met Daniel Free in 2003 on Maui, where we both walked our favorite beach. We soon became close friends. Daniel often spoke of his love for *A Course in Miracles,* the goal of which is to hear the Holy Spirit's Voice and follow His Guidance. Over the years, I have watched Daniel's progressive transformation, evidenced in this book of beautifully inspired poetry. He clearly expresses the love, clarity, and innocence of the Holy Spirit. As you read his offerings, you will tap right into your own Inner Voice, which will bring joy to your heart as it did mine. We are all One in God, and His Poetry lives in each of us. Daniel was willing to Ask for the experience of His Presence, has received it, and now wishes to share it with you.

Marjorie Tyler, Scribe of
One With God:
Awakening Through the Voice of the Holy Spirit
Books 1-8

God's Presence

Focus on God alone, and you are never alone.

I am here always and in all ways.

Introduction

These writings and poems
they came to me
now are written
to share with thee.

From His Presence,
deep inside,
in our hearts
He does reside.

His holy gifts,
comforting words,
in the Silence
they are heard.

To bring comfort
to bring peace
to bring love
to give release.

Release from pain,
release from hurt:
In God's Heart
we have our birth.

Born in God—
in Him alone,
in His Presence—
we are home.

The Door to God

We open the door to God by seeing our brother's innocence and remembering our own. It is the door to freedom, to Christ, to holiness; it is the door to God.

We open the door to God through a holy relationship; a relationship from the Holy Spirit, seeing the Holy Spirit in each other's eyes, in each other's heart; One Heart.

We each hold the key to the door; the key is kindness, forgiveness, seeing the sinlessness of each other, the perfection of each other, the perfection of all creation.

Home is where the heart is. Each of us longs to be loved, given compassion, kindness. God's gifts of love, kindness, and compassion are within each of us to give to each other; to share our hearts with the world.

Thoreau wrote, "Most men live lives of quiet desperation"—desperate for love, kindness, acceptance.

Love, kindness, acceptance appear missing in the world. Our world is missing holiness; our world is missing love; our world is missing aloha. This absence is felt in politics, on freeways, in business; this absence is felt in the battleground of ordinary life. This absence is seen in apparent terrorist attacks and war zones. A Loving Creator could never have created such a world. It is a dream. It is not real.

We have separated ourselves from our Creator and see a world that reflects His absence. In truth God is everywhere, ever present. In truth, His love is everywhere—ever present. Nowhere is God's Holy Presence absent.

We each have the power to bring God's Love to the world; to bring a love that is in the world but not of it. We each have the power to bring a healing to the world. It is within each of our hearts to be kind, loving, sensitive to others; to live our lives with kindness and compassion; to bring aloha to the world. It is in each of us to be God's instrument; it is in each of us to live a life that's holy.

A Holy Presence

A Holy Presence emanates from every soul, from the Heart of God to the heart of humanity; the Holy Christ Presence within everyone. No one is excluded.

Man has hidden his Holy Presence for eons, for lifetimes, like the movie *Groundhog Day*, the same scenario repeated with different costumes, different scenes, but always the same message; that each man is separate from his holy brother, separate from his holiness, from his Essence, from his Creator.

This is a holy time—a time of awakening—the day after Groundhog Day.

Chapter Thirty of the Text of *A Course in Miracles* is entitled "A New Beginning." This is a new beginning; a remembering of our Holy Christ Presence within—of remembering our unity with each other and with God.

The Quiet Bell

The Quiet Bell
makes no sound,
yet His Voice
is all around.

Loud and clear
His Voice is heard,
He speaks to us
in quiet words.

In every heart,
in every place,
His Quiet Voice
His Peace, His Grace.

God's Quiet Bell,
His Presence here –
In every heart –
His Voice so clear.

Now I Live

Now I live
with God's Grace.

Now I live
In a holy place.

Now I See

Now I see, everything clear.
Now I see, everything dear.

Now I see, One Soul.
Now I see, everything whole.

A New Vision – Our Boss Is God

I think of Michael Landon's character (an angel) on the television show *Highway to Heaven*—his Boss is God.

We have a choice which boss we listen to—the ego or God.

In Him, we live, move, and have our being. In Him we have holiness. In Him we have grace. In Him we have hope. In Him we have peace.

Christ in me, the Hope of Glory.

We can see through the ego's eyes and see a world of hopelessness and despair, or we can see the world with God's Vision and know a world of hope, grace, holiness, and peace.

In truth, we have One Boss, for we are One with God.

The Awakening

We are here to awaken. It is our only purpose; His holy plan. Humanity has been asleep for eons, since the beginning of time.

See the beauty in everyone, in all your brothers—for all are brothers— the Holy Sons of a Loving Father, a Loving God.

God is Pure. God is Holy. God is Love. Could we be different from our Creator?

His Voice awakens. His Spirit leads us home.

Hear the call for love in everyone, hidden in his heart. His heart cries for kindness, acceptance, forgiveness, for love.

See the beauty in his heart and know the beauty in your own.

The Title

A number of years ago, I was walking the Tiburon Bike Path. I walked this path almost every day for many years when I lived in Marin County. It is a beautiful place; the San Francisco Bay on one side, the hills of Tiburon on the other. It is a quiet place in the early morning; a place to feel the Peace, Grace, and the Love of God.

I have heard the expression, "you create your own reality," many times. It never felt true. Who is the you that is doing the creating? Is it the Christ Self we share with each other or the ego false self?

I have studied *A Course in Miracles* for many years. It is a book of awakening, awakening from the dream world of separation from each other and remembering we are one with each other and one with God; remembering only the Love of God expressing in and through his Holy Son is real.

The notion of separate reality is an illusion.

A Course in Miracles talks about the inversion of cause and effect. It says we are forever an Effect of God. If only God is real, or reality, then Reality Created Us. If God is Love, then Love Created Us, His One Son. We have invented a dream, a dream which is not real.

I thought about *Reality Created Us* as the title of a book. The Holy Spirit gave me the words, *Love Created Us.*

Many years later, I was walking the same Tiburon Bike Path. I had not yet written the book. There was more to the title, more to the book. He gave me the words, *Living a Life That's Holy*, and I knew that was the rest of the title of the book.

Love Created Us; Living a Life That's Holy

We were created by Love, the Holy Son of God, designed to live according to His plan for our lives.

His plan is one of joy, peace, and love. It is a reflection of the Love of God on this earth.

Every part of His Kingdom is holy, for it is an expression and reflection of His Love; the Heart of God is within all. It encompasses His Kingdom—a Kingdom filled with His Love.

The world as seen through the eyes of the ego has reflected pain, sorrow, loss, and fear. It is a world of sorrow. It is not a reflection of the Kingdom of God.

Man believes he creates his own reality; a reality that is separate from his brothers, a reality that is separate from God.

This apparent reality is a dream, a nightmare, an illusion. It is a reflection of an angry, capricious god made manifest. It is a nightmare, a dream, an illusion, for it does not reflect the Loving Presence of the Divine. It does not reflect the Loving Presence of a Loving God. It is a world of apparent separation from our Reality, from our Source, from the Loving Presence of God. It is not real.

The belief that you create your own reality is the lie that shapes the dreamworld.

Only God is real. God is Love. His Reality expresses only Love. It is pure. It is holy. It is kind. It is a world of peace, for it reflects only His Love.

Releasing Dynamism

Man appears to live in a dynamic universe, a universe of constant change, constant flux. It is not real. In the Holy Instant, man remembers Who He is, for he is the Holy Son of God.

Eckhart Tolle wrote a book called *The Power of Now* and another called *Stillness Speaks*. Man mistakenly believes vibration speaks. It is the echo; stillness is the song. God, the Holy Spirit, uses the universe we have invented for a holy purpose; to bring His Son home. He is the Conductor, the Maestro. He orchestrates the dream world for a holy purpose. $E=mc^2$, Einstein's famous equation of the relationship between matter and energy. Einstein also discovered the Law of Conservation of Energy; Energy (or matter) cannot be created or destroyed. If you leave off the last two words of this statement, there is a profound realization; energy (or matter) cannot be created. It is a dream. It is not real.

There is a lesson in *A Course in Miracles*; "I have invented the world I see" (W-p1.32). It is a dynamic universe. The Kingdom of God is Still; God's changeless dwelling place; a place of quiet, of rest, of peace, joy, and happiness that lies beyond this world. For it is the home of God and His Holy Son. Our Holy Christ Presence is Still.

Jesus knew and lived this lesson from *A Course in Miracles*; "I am not a body; I am free, for I am still as God created me" (W-p1.218). The frequency and vibration of Jesus' body was higher than that of others. The Stillness in his heart was the same. He recognized the same Stillness in him is the same Stillness in his brothers. Through this recognition, he was—and is—able to reach, touch, and heal everyone. Our vibration naturally rises as we come to know our Creator. It is the echo; stillness is the song. This is a lesson in *A Course in Miracles*; "I will be still an instant and go home" (W-p1.182). The Still Small Voice leads us home.

The Holy Presence

I am sitting at home, alone,
But not alone.
A Holy Presence
Beyond time-yet in all time
Beyond space-yet in all space
Beyond form-yet in all form
A Holy Presence in unholy places
making them holy.

The Light arisen
The Holy Christ is born in me today,
making all unholy places holy,
One with God.
The Holy Presence heals my heart.
The Holy Presence heals the heart of humanity.

God's Love Reflected
The Holy Christ Presence

The Holy Spirit uses the world for our awakening. He uses the world for a holy purpose—to bring us home to our Source—to bring us home to our Christ Presence.

The world of frequency and vibration is not real—it is a dream of separation from our Source. But it can be used by God for the Great Awakening—for a holy purpose.

The world was not created by God, for it is a world of apparent beginnings and endings, of time, of space. It is temporal. The Kingdom of God is forever.

Yet He can bring the Holy Christ Presence to all we see, touch, and hear. The world of form, time, and space can reflect the temporal—or it can reflect the Holy Christ Presence that is always in our hearts, for our hearts and the Heart of God are One.

God has One Son. His Son is holy.

Our life on earth can be lived by Him. Our life can reflect the peace, love, and grace of our Creator.

The music of the spheres is celestial. We can use the world of frequency and vibration to reflect and express the Still Small Voice of God. We can see it everywhere and in everyone, for it is everywhere and in everyone. There is not a place, person, or time without the Holy Christ Presence, for we are the Holy Christ Presence. We are God's Son.

Love's Reflection

God's plan for the Great Awakening is gentle, loving, and kind. It is holy—as is His Son.

The ego's world is a world of dreams, a world of apparent pain, suffering, and death.

Would a Loving God create a world of pain, suffering, and death? Would a God of pure love allow His Son to suffer? Would a Loving God cause pain to His Son? Could the Source of Eternal Life create a world of pain, suffering, and death? There are three beautiful lessons of God's Truth in *A Course in Miracles,* "I can be free of suffering today" (W-p2.340); "God's Will for me is perfect happiness" (W- p1.101); "There is no death, the Son of God is free" (W-p1.163).

Either God isn't loving, or the ego's world—a world of pain, suffering, and death—is not real. It is a dream. God is Love. His Son, Our Holy Christ Presence, is His Essence in Creation; a Creation of joy, of peace, of love.

We are as pure as our Creator. We are as holy as our Creator. We are One with our Source—One with God—One with Love. We are love.

Love's reflection is in the world, for it is in our hearts, one with God's Heart. We can live from this holy place and bring the holiness of our Creator to everyone and everything, for it is in everyone and everything.

This is the Great Awakening. We can see the truth. We can remember we are one with God.

Where Is God?

Where is God? Where is God not? In the world of dreams, God is here. His Son is never alone, never without His help.

God's helpers are all around you, surrounding you with His Love, holding you safe forever in His Loving Arms.

His Hand reaches for you. His Heart is one with your heart, for you are one with Him, one with your Creator—as holy as He is.

You are never without His Love. You are never without His Embrace.

God knows not pain and suffering. He knows only love. He is only love.

God is Always There

Sometimes the words don't come. Sometimes the words flow. God is in the words. God is in the pauses. He is in the space between the notes. The space is God. The space is Love. There is a holy plan for everyone. He carries us home.

There is a story of a man who would see his footprints on the ground. Sometimes he would see another set of footprints—God's. Sometimes, when he felt most troubled, most abandoned, most alone, he saw only one set of footprints.

He said to God, pointing at the one set of footprints, "Why have You abandoned me when I most needed You?"

God answered, "That is when I carried you."

We are never alone, never abandoned by our Holy Source, for we are one with Him who loves and cares for us. We are the Holy Christ Presence. We are God's Son.

We can dream we are alone, abandoned by our Creator. We dream until we awaken to the truth—we are always one with our Creator, our Source. We are one with God.

We can see His Love reflected in our hearts. We can see the Holy Christ Presence in each of our brothers. We can see the truth, know the truth, feel the truth, and know we are one with God.

Each one carries that spark, that light, in his heart. Sometimes it is hidden, hidden in the pain, shame, guilt. It is seen through forgiveness. It is seen through loving eyes. It is felt with a loving heart. We can awaken. We are awakening. We are coming home.

Remembering Our Innocence

I was taking a nap. I felt I should be doing something more productive—writing. Then I saw the truth; my innocence.

I thought of the Bible passage about the lilies of the field; they neither toil nor spin.

I saw and felt the sacredness of rest—the holiness of rest.

There is a beautiful lesson in *A Course in Miracles* entitled, "I rest in God" (W-p1.109). It is a lesson about being refreshed. It is the gift of renewal.

I remembered my innocence as I rested in God. I allowed His Holy Presence to come to me—to come through me.

Our work can be holy. Our work is holy—sharing God's Love through our thoughts, words and deeds—seeing the innocence in ourselves and in everyone.

We have been asleep, living in a world of dreams; a world that is not real. Yet even here, we can have the Kingdom of God reflected in our lives. We can hold the Kingdom of God in our hearts.

We can awaken. We can let go. We can live a life that's holy, for we are the Holy Son of God.

We can rest in His Loving Embrace. We can rest in our innocence. We can rest.

Remembering

We are here to awaken, awaken from the dream of the world—a world of despair, loneliness, and separation—and know it is not real. It is a dream. Would a loving God have created a world of despair, loneliness, suffering, and separation for His Creation, His Son?

God is only love. We are created in His image. Therefore, we must be only love.

We can forgive and see our innocence reflected in everyone. In truth, our innocence is ever-present.

Kindness is the bridge from the world we made to the Kingdom of God, a place of peace, joy, and love, and remembering our unity with our Creator and all creation.

We can bring the Kingdom of God to everyone. We can bring it everywhere. It is the holy place in our hearts.

We can remember who we are. We can awaken. We can know we are love and live a life that's holy.

The Call for Love

The call for love is ever present, for love is forever present; love is.

Love is the only sane response to the appearance of pain and suffering, for love heals all pain and suffering; love heals.

God is Love. We were created with the same Essence as our Creator. We are love. Many have forgotten Our Holy Essence.

Lack of love shows in the insanity of the world. From speeding on freeways to holocausts, many have forgotten our connection with each other, our connection with our holiness, our connection with God.

We can bring our holiness to the world, for we were created holy. We can bring our love to the world, for we were created in love, as love.

Insanity has been defined as doing the same thing over and over and expecting a different result.

We can begin anew. We can be God's instruments of healing. We can bring salvation to the world.

Who is the Maestro, the Conductor?

We have a choice which voice we will listen to—the voice of the world or the Voice for God? One Voice, the Voice for God, brings us love, kindness, joy, peace. Only God's Voice is real.

The other voice, the voice of the ego, brings us pain, suffering, despair, and death for it is the voice of pain, suffering, despair, and death.

It is the voice of the world, a world we have made, but surely not one a loving God would have created for His Son. Yet we can bring God's Love even here, for we carry the Love of God in our hearts. We can see everything as an expression of His Love, or a call for help, a call for God's Loving Hands, a call for love.

We can extend the Love of God to everyone, holding everyone in God's Embrace, holding everyone in a holy place of love.

We are God's instruments. He is the Maestro, the Conductor. We bring salvation to the world.

God Gives the Words

What do we have to say? What does God have to say? God says everything for He is everything.

His Holy Presence encompasses humanity. His Holy Presence enfolds creation. All is held in His Loving Embrace, all creation held in His Heart, all humanity enfolded with His Love.

He knows what words to give each brother; words of comfort, healing, and love.

His Words touch the heart of everyone for He is in the heart of everyone.

God sees the call for love in apparent pain and suffering. His Love is the balm that soothes, that heals, that blesses humanity.

His Holy Presence is made known to His Creation, His Son. The holiness of all creation in revealed. Holiness is restored to humanity.

Listening to God

I am here, everywhere, in every person, place, circumstance in which you find yourself. Every decision is an opportunity to awaken.

Viktor Frankl wrote *Man's Search for Meaning* while in a concentration camp. He was able to experience the Presence of God in a concentration camp because God was present in his heart.

God is always present, present in the heart of humanity, in everyone's heart, in all places, times.

Even what appears ordinary can be seen with God's Vision. Every person can be seen with love. Every person wants love, dignity, respect, kindness.

Every person has a story. Mr. Fred Rogers, the host of the PBS show *Mr. Roger's Neighborhood,* once heard the words, "There is no one you couldn't love if you only knew their story." The truth in these words stayed with him the rest of his life. He saw the call for love beneath the pain, beneath the apparent toughness, beneath the heart that appears hardened.

Just as heat can melt butter, a kind heart touches everyone, blesses everyone. Kindness and forgiveness bless the giver and receiver, for the giver and receiver are one.

We can love, for we are love. There is a beautiful lesson from *A Course in Miracles,* "Love created me like itself" (W-p1.67) and "Holiness created me holy. Kindness created me kind" (W-p1.67.2:3,4). Our Creator is holy. Our Creator is kindness. Our Creator is love.

We were created in God's image. Anything else (hurt, pain, suffering) is a call for love, a call for kindness. Love and kindness heal our souls. Love and kindness bring healing to our world. Love and kindness awaken us from the dream of separation and reveal our unity with each other and that we are one with God.

Remembering Innocence

Innocence can be revealed, for it is a revelation—a revelation of hope, of kindness, of grace, of love.

Innocence can be felt in all places and times, for it is in all places and times. Innocence is in our hearts; our hearts are innocent.

Viktor Frankl brought the holiness of God's Vision to a concentration camp. We can bring the Love of God everywhere, for it is everywhere.

Jesus knew his innocence when he was being judged. He saw the innocence in all his brothers. His words to God were, "Forgive them, Father, for they know not what they do."

We can remember. We can know the truth. We can see as Jesus sees. We can see.

We can see the innocence in each brother, see what they may have forgotten.

We can see the truth. We can know the truth. We can be God's holy messengers of love, of kindness.

We can awaken from the dream and live from a holy place of love, being a spotless mirror, bringing God's Light to humanity.

Seeing

I was taking a walk in the afternoon. I was feeling sad, feeling alone. I saw trees, houses, cars, the sights of the world. Then I saw with God's Eyes—saw the truth. I am holy. So is everyone.

How can we not be? We were created by Love, by Holiness, by God. If we were created in the image of our Creator, how can we not be holy?

I saw with vision, saw God's holiness reflected everywhere, because it is everywhere.

All of humanity, all of us are holy. We have a holy purpose. We are never alone for we are one with each other, one with God. We are God's Son.

Our Journey Home

Our journey home is a journey of remembrance, remembering Who we are, that we are the Holy Son of God. One lesson in *A Course in Miracles* is, "I am the Holy Son of God Himself" (W-p1.191). It is about remembering Our Christ Essence, remembering our holiness, remembering we are one with God.

Our journey home is holy. Every step is guided by the Holy Spirit. Our path is blessed, sacred. He shows the Way for He is the Way, the Truth, and the Life. Another *Course* lesson is, "Father, I will but to remember You" (W-p2.231). What can be holier than remembering God? What can be holier than coming home?

In truth, we have never left our Source. Only in dreams could we appear separate from our brothers, separate from God. We can awaken. We can remember. We can come home.

The Grace of God

There is a beautiful quote from *A Course in Miracles,* "Let me remember I am one with God, at one with all my brothers and my Self, in everlasting holiness and peace" (W-p1.124.12:2). The Grace of God is holy. It brings us home, gives us peace, sustains our souls. The Grace of God touches our hearts, for it is in our hearts.

Sometimes it appears covered over by circumstances, by the world, but we can awaken and know the Grace of God is always present in our hearts.

We can bring the light that shines away apparent darkness. We can bring God's Grace to circumstances, situations, and places that appear unholy and bring holiness everywhere for it is everywhere. In truth, there is no place, circumstance, or time untouched by God's Holy Presence. Viktor Frankl felt the Presence of God in a concentration camp. He carried it in his heart.

We can bring this holy presence to all our brothers. We can awaken and know the Grace of God. We can be at peace. We can rest in God's Loving Arms. We can live lives that are holy for we are holy; the holy Son of a loving Father.

We can know the truth; our Essence touches others because, in reality, there are no others. We are one; one with each other, one with God.

Renewal

God's Kingdom is always here. It is ever-present in our hearts.

We can heal all suffering, heal all pain by seeing our brother's innocence. We will then know our own.

We have never left the Kingdom of God. Only in dreams have we left His Kingdom.

Just as library book can be renewed without penalty, we can know the love that is already in our hearts. There are no late fees, no fines. It is fine to come home; we are already here. Just as the Prodigal Son was welcomed home by his father, we will be welcomed home by God. One lesson from *A Course in Miracles* is, "Forgiveness is the key to happiness" (W-p1.121). This morning I saw my brother's innocence. This morning, I felt my own.

There is joy in the Kingdom. There is joy in my heart. There is joy in every Son of God, for we were created in joy, in love.

God's Answer Alone

"God's answer is some form of peace" (W-p2.359)—God's peace. God's answer is kind to everyone. God's answer brings healing to humanity. His direction suffices. The Holy Spirit gently guides us with His love.

Man asks many questions. God answers. God's answer brings a holy, loving, and kind answer to every question because God is holy, loving, and kind. God's answer brings salvation.

There is a beautiful prayer from *A Course in Miracles,* "What would You have me do? Where would You have me go? What would You have me say—and to whom?" (W-p1.71.9:3-5).

He knows the answer. He is the answer. He guides each of us home. All we need do is call on Him. All we need do is be still. All we need do is listen to His Voice.

He will answer.

A Holy Place

God's Presence is holy. We remember His Presence when we take time to be with Him, make space for Him in our lives—in our hearts. He is always here.

There is a beautiful book called *God Calling*. Two women heard God's Voice, the Voice of Jesus, and wrote what they received. From the message, "In My Presence," (February 14) they were given the message that by keeping time apart with Me they are being, "transformed physically, mentally, spiritually into My likeness," and by remembering Me they are bringing My Presence to all they meet and, "making one spot on earth a Holy Place."

We can remember. We can awaken. We can remember our Holy Christ Presence. We can awaken the Holy Christ Presence in all humanity and bring holiness to the world.

We can touch others, bless others. We can bring healing to the world. We are the bringers of salvation. This is our purpose. Our love can shine a light into darkened spaces, bringing God's Light—God's Love—to everyone.

We can be kind, loving. We were created kind and loving by a kind and loving God. We can know the truth. The truth shall set us free. The truth in us is awakening humanity, bringing us home to God.

Finding Your Roots

There is a television show on PBS with Henry Louis Gates Jr. called *Finding Your Roots*. It is about guests on the show meeting their ancestors and knowing their heritage.

While discovering their ancestors' journeys, their struggles, their traumas, their overcoming obstacles, many guest and viewers have been touched. We all have roots that go far deeper and can touch us in a far deeper way; our Divine Heritage. We find our real roots—the holy ground on which we stand—when we remember; remember our connection with everyone whether biologically related or not. We find our real roots when we remember God.

We have been uprooted for eons. We have forgotten our Source, our Essence. We are holy. We are God's Son. Our roots connect us to our Source. We are rooted in God.

Living in His Presence

The Presence of God is holy, loving, and kind. When we enter into His Presence, we remember our Essence; we remember that we are holy, loving, and kind. We can see the world anew. We can see everyone with eyes of love, eyes of kindness. We can live with a loving heart for our hearts are loving; our hearts are kind.

We can see the world as Jesus' saw; saw with eyes of kindness, saw with a heart of love.

The loving God that created Jesus created us—created us like Him, as Him.

There is a beautiful section in lesson 157 of *A Course in Miracles*, "Into Christ's Presence will we enter now, serenely unaware of everything except His shining face and perfect Love" (W-p1.157.9:1).

We can awaken. We can remember. We can live in the Presence of God.

We can bring this Holy Christ Presence to all we meet; it is in everyone. We can see the truth, know the truth, be the truth, live the truth.

We can live lives that are holy. We were created holy by God's Loving Hands; we live in His Heart.

Releasing Illusions

"All the world's a stage." These are William Shakespeare's famous words from his play *As You Like It*. That is the one truth of the world; it is not real.

Would God have created such a world for His Holy Son; a world of pain, suffering, sadness, and terror, a world of loss, a world of insanity? Since the world is not a loving place, either God isn't loving or the world is not real. Clearly, this world was not created by a loving God.

The world is valueless because it is a dream; it is not real. How can a false world be the Kingdom of God?

Yet we can bring the Kingdom of God everywhere. We can bring God's Love to everyone we meet or think of. We can be in this world but not of it because in reality we are not of this world; we are God's Holy Son.

The Holy Christ Presence abides in everyone.

We are the bringers of salvation. We can bring God's Love for we were created in love. We can bring God's Light, happiness, and peace for we were created with the light, happiness, and peace of our Creator.

We can bring hope. We can bring healing. We are God's instruments of salvation.

I Had a Dream

This was not the kind of dream Dr. Martin Luther King Jr. had when he gave his famous speech.

It was a dream about recharging my computer—at a gas station. I was at the gas station and got busy on the computer and with other things. I could not remember whether or not I had paid for gas. I asked the attendant and he said I did. I was about to put gas in my car when I awoke.

When I awoke, I remembered I was charging my computer overnight. When I awoke, I remembered—remembered the truth. A charged battery keeps the computer operational. A filled gas tank keeps the car going. Air, sunlight, food, and water are fuel for our bodies. We are sustained by our connection with our Source; we are sustained by God's Love. We have been using the ego's fuel of pain and separation from a loving God and from each other for eons. This nonsense only makes sense in dreams.

There is a lesson in *A Course in Miracles*, "I am sustained by the Love of God" (W-p1.50). Taking time to remember our connection with God sustains us. Remembering our connection with our Source is the air, the sunlight, the food, and water for our hearts, our Essence.

Our connection with God is essential. It brings us peace. Another *Course* lesson is, "I will be still an instant and go home" (W-p1.182). Taking time to be still, to be with God, sustains us. Remembering our connection with our Source and with each other brings us home.

In the Silence

In the silence there is grace.
In the silence, a holy place.

In the silence, God is here.
In the silence all is clear.

In the silence, there is no thrill.
In the silence is God's Will.

In the silence there is no race.
Only each brother's holy face.

In the silence there is no place
The world disappears without a trace.

In the silence there is no time.
In the silence, no bells chime.

In the silence, a holy place.
In the silence, see God's Face.

Where is the Meaning of Life?

People have asked what is the meaning of life? Is there meaning in a dream? Can God's Son find solace in illusions?

We are here to awaken—to wake up from a dream of pain and suffering and have God's peace, love, and joy.

"Where is the meaning of life?" may be a more useful question. One lesson in *A Course in Miracles* is, "My meaningless thoughts are showing me a meaningless world" (W-p1.11). Life has no external meaning for the life of God is in our hearts. We carry God's Essence in our souls for we are God's Essence, the Holy Christ Presence that is in us all.

We can see with God's Vision. We can see with God's Heart. We can see the world anew: fresh, clean, holy.

God's Love is Everywhere

God's Love is everywhere because God is everywhere. God is ever-present. God is forever present. There is no space, time, or circumstance where God is not.

God is present in apparent pain and suffering but He is never the cause. His Holy Presence is the release of apparent pain and suffering, which God never created nor intended for His Son.

It is a nightmare. It is not real, though it can appear very real. A Loving God would never have created a nightmare for His Son. All that is real is God's Creation. All that is real is God's Love.

We can see the Love of God reflected in nature for it is natural. We can see God's Love reflected in the beauty of trees, flowers, mountains, the ocean. We can see the Love of God reflected in each other's kindness, in music, in literature, in art, in science. We can see His Love reflected everywhere for it is everywhere.

Even in places of apparent misery such as sweatshops, prisons, and concentration camps we can bring God's Holy Presence; we can bring kindness, beauty, and grace. We can abolish such places by finding the Love of God within our hearts, living with His Vision, seeing with His Vision.

He does not bring pain and suffering to His Son. He brings only love, only kindness. His Presence is our salvation.

We can awaken from the nightmare of pain and suffering and live in our true home, God's Kingdom, a place of love, of grace, of joy, of happiness, of peace. This is His Will for His Son. Our illusions, our dreams, have hidden His Kingdom from eons. It has always been here. We can see it more and more as our awakening deepens. We can live more and more in God's Holy Presence and bring His Love to all we meet.

We can become, as *A Course in Miracles* says, "A spotless mirror, in which the Holiness of your Creator shines forth" (T-14.IX.5:1). Our lives can reflect holiness for we were created holy. Our lives can reflect kindness for we were created kind. Our lives can reflect love for we were created by Love, by His Loving Hands.

We have a holy purpose; to awaken, to remember Him. We are the bringers of salvation—His instruments.

The Deepest Part

The deepest part
is inside my heart.
Touching God,
It is not hard.

Being here
holding my brothers dear.
Before the fall
all was one.
To come home again,
our journey done.

Having peace,
the sweet release.
Free at last,
the past has passed.

Withdrawal

This evening I have been going through withdrawal—withdrawal from the world.

It has not been a comfortable ride, yet I know it is a ride to comfort; to being at home with the Divine Comforter, to being at home.

Sleep can give the appearance of comfort. Sleep can only comfort in dreams.

It is wake-up time. TV, computers, all the distractions of the world can be detours. Like the bells and noise in a casino, they can appear exciting—until the emptiness is felt.

Feeling the emptiness can appear painful. It is, however, the road to salvation. It is the pathway home.

The glitter of the world has bound God's Son for eons. It has kept Him in chains.

Feeling the emptiness of the world brings us one step closer to feeling the richness of God's Kingdom—a place of peace, grace, joy, and love that is not of this world but is the essence of our true home, the essence of our souls—the Essence of God.

He Always Holds Our Hand

We are never alone, never without help.

I had a dream about a couple holding hands. They appreciated each other, loved each other, and supported each other on their journey through a forest, their journey home.

God is always reaching out His Hand. All we need is to take hold of His Hand for He always holds our hand and He will lead us home.

Building a Foundation

In the Bible, there is a passage about building a house on a firm foundation of solid rock instead of shifting sands. The house built on shifting sands is blown away in a storm. The house built on solid rock remains.

The appearances of the world are like shifting sands. They can morph and change into appearances we like and then change in an instant into a nightmare. The world is not a solid foundation for God's Son for it is not His real home.

We do not need to build a foundation. It is the Kingdom of God, our true home. He has built the foundation. Like the Prodigal Son, we need to come home.

In truth, we have never left our home. We have been, "at home in God dreaming of exile" (T-10. I,2:1). We have left our home only in dreams.

We can awaken. We can remember. We can, "be still an instant and go home" (W-p1.182).

Bringers of Salvation

Everyone wants their lives to matter yet we are not matter. Everyone wants to make a difference yet we are not different.

We are essential for we share God's Essence. We are holy. We are part of the whole yet contain the whole. The ocean is embodied in the wave, in each drop of water.

Lesson 100 in *A Course in Miracles* is entitled. "My part is essential for God's plan for salvation." I want to share a paragraph of this lesson with you:

"You are indeed essential to God's plan. Just as your light increases every light that shines in Heaven, so your joy on earth calls to all minds to let their sorrows go, and take their place besides you in God's plan. God's messengers are joyous, and their joy heals sorrow and despair. They are proof that God wills perfect happiness for all who will accept their Father's gifts as theirs" (W-p1.100.4:1-4).

We make a difference not because we are different but because we are the same; we are God's One Son. Our Holy Christ Presence shines God's Light into the world. We are God's messengers of love, of kindness, of joy.

We are the bringers of salvation. We turn a world of apparent matter—of apparent differences—into the Kingdom of God, our true home in Him. We remember our unity with each other and with our Creator by remembering there are no differences, and that form is an illusion. We are spirit, whole, holy. We bring salvation to the world.

His Words Alone

With His Words, we are never alone.

My friend Margie Tyler woke-up at three one morning several years ago and heard the word *Write*. She did.

She woke-up hearing the Voice of the Holy Spirit. She awoke. Margie is not special. Each of us can hear His Voice because His Holy Presence is deep within our hearts.

We can hear God speak through His Words. We can feel the Presence of God in music. We can feel His Presence in nature, by the ocean, on the earth. We can feel His Presence in the Silence.

We can see the Presence of God in each other for His Presence is in all His Sons, no matter the outward appearance. In God's Kingdom, there are no outward appearances for there are no appearances, only Reality, only Love.

The Kingdom of God is not outside. It is within us all. We can live in a world that reflects His love for we were created in love. We can bring love to the world for we are love.

In God's Embrace

In God's Embrace,
all pain erased.
No more to roam
for we are home.

In God's Embrace,
the truth revealed.
In God's Embrace,
His Son is healed.

In God's Embrace,
from above
His Son received,
received in love.

In God's Embrace,
the long journey done.
In God's Embrace,
We have come home.

Feeling God's Embrace

Last night, I was feeling a deep sadness—feeling sad, feeling alone. I was feeling. Feeling brings healing.

I was not numb but feeling what I had numbed for eons, for lifetimes. I was in the process of a deep soul renewal and healing.

I had forgotten God's Embrace. I had forgotten. Now I remember. I feel His Embrace; I feel His Love.

We are all connected with each other and with our Creator. This is the truth.

The world has been home to pain, sadness, suffering, and apparent separation for eons.

Now is the time to feel. Now is the time to awaken. Now is the time to feel the Love of God in our hearts.

It is all that is real in the world.

Our Sight Restored

There is a story in the Bible of a man who could not see but had his sight restored by Jesus. He could then see.

What are we seeing? Are we seeing the Presence of God or the illusions of the world? Only His Presence is real.

The illusions of the world are just that—illusions. When we see illusions, the truth is hidden from our eyes, from our hearts, from our sight.

Now is the time to have our sight restored; to see the beauty in each other, to see with love, with kindness.

Now is the time to see.

Our Life in God is Not a Daring Adventure

There is a famous quote from Helen Keller; "Life is a daring adventure or nothing."

Man has gone on many daring adventures for lifetimes, for eons. All they have brought is pain, suffering and heartache. They are a dream; they are not real. The daring adventures of the ego have brought us nothing, because they are nothing.

There is a lesson in *A Course in Miracles*; "There is one life and that I share with God" (W-p1.167). Our life with God brings us everything, because it is everything. It is a place of quiet, rest, stillness, grace and peace. It is a place of love.

There is a beautiful section of *A Course in Miracle* called The Real Alternative; "Real choice is no illusion. But the world has none to offer. All its roads but lead to disappointment, nothingness and death . . . . The roads this world can offer seem to be quite large in number, but the time must come when everyone must begin to see how like they are to one another" (T-31.IV.2,3:1-3,3).

There is a real alternative; God's path. It is no daring adventure. It is everything, for it leads us home. It brings us peace.

We can be in this world but not of it, for in truth, we are in the world but not of it.

Like everyone, the Prodigal Son went on a daring adventure. It brought him pain, suffering and despair. Then he chose to come home.

Like the Prodigal Son, we can go on daring adventures which bring us nothing. Or we can awaken. We can come home. We can have the Peace of God.

Leap of Faith

"Most men live lives of quiet desperation"; Thoreau's well-known quote. Most men live lives of quiet desperation because they don't live lives of quiet.

There is a difference between daring and dancing. One is a useless journey; the other brings us home.

Who is our partner in the dance of life? Hildegard of Bingen, the twelfth-century Benedictine nun, was an artist, writer, visionary and composer of sacred music. She was named Doctor of the Catholic Church, one of only 39 people (including just 4 women) to be so honored. Hildegard of Bingen danced. She danced with God.

We can dance with each other, move with each other, be still, silent with each other and know the Grace of God.

We can hold each other's hearts, hold each other as to sacred, have holy relationships filled with peace, love and joy which bring us home to God.

There is joy in the Kingdom, joy in our souls, joy in our hearts.

In Him we live, move and have our being. In Him we are home.

We can take the leap of faith and know we will by caught, embraced with love. We can bring God's Love to everyone by sharing the love in our hearts.

The ego goes on daring adventures. A leap of faith brings us home.

What Are We Breathing?

I awoke this morning and prayed, exercised and stretched and breathed. I breathed in the morning air; the breath of life. I breathed in freshness, renewal, aloha; the Breath of God.

For eons, man has been breathing the toxic fumes of the ego, of judgements, suffering and pain. Now is the time for a breath of fresh air, to awaken, to breathe.

Clean Air is our salvation. It is His Breath of love, kindness and forgiveness. His Breath, His Air is essential for our lives and well-being. It is our Essence. It is the gift of aloha.

The Journey Alone, or the Journey Home

In truth, we are never alone. In Him we live move and have our being. In Him we are home.

We only journey alone in dreams. God goes with us always. He is always here, our Rock, our Redeemer. In Him we live.

We have been taking the long way home for eons, for lifetimes. Now is the time to remember, remember our holiness, remember our Divine heritage. Our Creator is Holy. How can we not be holy, when we were created by His Loving Hands, and the Love of God infuses our hearts?

We breathe aloha, live aloha, are aloha. In truth, we are never alone. God is always present—ever present. It is time to awaken, time to remember, to know we are home in the Kingdom of God.

With God's Love

With God's Love,
the truth revealed,
the message heard,
the Door unsealed.

The Light now shines
the Master's Hand,
freedom chimes
the Master's plan.

With God's Love,
Amazing Grace,
in His Arms
we are embraced.

With His Love,
His Kingdom has come;
we are home,
the journey done.

God Speaks to Thee

In the silence
beyond the words,
In the silence,
God's Voice is heard.

On the mountain,
by the sea,
God will always speak to thee.

In each brother,
His Voice is heard,
If you can see
beyond his words.

See his soul,
his call for love,
Share His Presence
like a dove.

See his soul,
know his heart,
for you and he
are not apart.

At home or on the road
His Holy Presence will enfold—
enfold our hearts,
enfold our soul;
His message is forever told.

His message is forever heard.
His Voice heals the world.

God speaks to thee,
To you and me;
His Presence known,
His Presence shown.

On Holy Ground

We stand on Holy Ground. We stand on His Shoulders. We rest in His Arms.

We are always in His Presence for we are His Presence; His Presence is in us as we are in God. His Love surrounds us, showing the way.

I was inspired by today's (March 6) message from a beautiful book called *God Calling* by Two Listeners. The message was entitled, "Love and Laughter."

God is the fertile soil for His Creation, His One Son. We sprout in and with his Love.

We can plant holy seeds in fertile soil. We can create with and through our love.

We can plant in fertile soil; the fertile soil of love, kindness, forgiveness.

We can have faith and know our seeds will sprout and flowers of love, kindness, grace, and beauty will bloom.

We can plant seeds in fertile soil. We plant on Holy Ground.

Heaven's Gate is Always Open

I went on a hike this morning. The day was beautiful, the air clear. There were trees, wildflowers, the sounds of nature, the silence of nature.

I came upon a gate. It was closed, locked. It has a purpose; to keep people out.

Heaven's Gate has another purpose—a holy purpose—to welcome God's Son home.

It is always open for it is an opening. It is a doorway to Heaven. It is the entrance to our true home.

All God's Children are welcome. No one is barred. The entrance is one of kindness, grace, and beauty. The entrance is one of love.

All may enter here. God loves everyone. It is a holy place—The Holy Christ Presence in our hearts. All our errors are forgiven, erased, undone.

God's Light is shining, welcoming. It is a place of grace in all creation. It is a place of love.

Heaven's Gate is always open, as we open our hearts to love.

The Truth Revealed

The truth revealed
God's Son is healed,
not led astray
but home to stay.

The door opens
to Heaven above,
above the world
a place of love.

To live in joy,
to know God's Grace,
to fly with wings
to a holy place.

A holy place
where God resides,
A holy place
God does not hide.

The truth revealed,
the layers peeled.
The sun's now here
for His Son so dear.

With His Love
The Light now shines;
A Holy Presence,
God's Presence Divine.

The truth revealed,
No more concealed
with glory bright—
seen with God's Sight.

With God's Love
the dream released,
The Son of God
now finds God's peace.

The Same Truth Abides in Everyone

There is a well-known statement, "There is no 'I' in team." That is the "I" of the ego; it is not the Eye of God.

The Eyes of God hold the truth. With the Eyes of God, we see the truth, know the truth, live the truth, are the truth.

Just as a team is one, united, the same truth abides in everyone. *A Course in Miracles* states that one lie is the belief that truth is different for everyone. How can truth be different for everyone when we are the same, when we are one, the One Son of God?

God's truth is in all His Sons; it is ever-present, holy. The same truth abides in everyone for we are one with each other; we are One with God.

His Holy Presence

His Holy Presence
now is here.
The Light of God
now shines clear.

The Face of Christ, in each other's eyes
no longer hidden by a thin disguise.

The Heart of God is now seen,
once hidden by a senseless dream.

The dream of terror, so long endured,
God answers with His Holy Cure.

His Holy Cure
seen with God's Sight,
His Holy Light
now so bright.

Christ's gentle eyes
now revealed,
no longer hidden,
no more concealed.

His Presence seen,
the dream undone;
no more dreams
for His Holy Son.

Sweet Release

Sweet release
bringing peace.
It's not hard
to be one with God.

The sun shines bright,
there is no night,
only joy;
His Son's birthright.

With Heaven's Gate,
no sadness here,
no more to wait;
God's Joy now clear.

No more lament,
our soul's content;
only joy, seen with His Sight;
only joy, our sweet delight.

Sweet release
His Son at peace.
Living Water flows
where God's Son goes.

Detachment—Connection

When we detach from the world, we remember our connection with God. We awaken. In reality, attachment is a dream. How can God's Son be attached to anybody or anything when nothing in the world of form is permanent; it has no substance, it is not real?

Attachment is a cover for what we really want; to remember our deep connection with each other, to remember our deep connection with God. This connection is deep within our souls, deep within our hearts.

This connection is holy, sacred. It is God's Living Water in all of His Creation. When we detach from the world of dreams, when we let go, we remember the truth; we awaken. We awaken and know our connection with each other, our connection with God.

The Holy Ghost Will Never Ghost Us

The Holy Ghost will never ghost us. In the dream, we have appeared to have ghosted God.

We have invented a world of separation from each other and from our Source. It is a world of dreams. We believe we have invented a place where the Holy Loving Presence of God could enter not. It is a fantasy, a nightmare, an illusion. Only God's Kingdom is real. We are the ones who have ghosted God.

In the world of dreams, we appear to be separate from each other and from our Creator. Appearances are not truth. In reality, we have never left our Source.

Humanity's guilt and projection of that guilt onto others is mirrored in the practice of ghosting—not answering texts or calls—projecting our guilt onto our brothers.

God knows our innocence. He calls us home. Will we continue to ghost our Creator or will we answer His Call?

A New Filling

Yesterday, I drove to see my dentist to have a broken filling replaced. It was a long drive, there and back. It was well-worth it. My dentist and her staff worked with kindness and love. My tooth was made whole, restored.

For eons, mankind has been filling the emptiness in our souls and hearts with what has filled the world; the ego's gifts of pain and despair. This is what has filled the world. It is not God's plan for His Son.

Now is the time for a new filling. Now is the time to fill our hearts with love, kindness, forgiveness.

In truth, love and kindness are deep within our hearts, our souls.

Just as a dentist cleans our teeth and removes the old filling, we can cleanse our hearts through forgiveness, seeing our innocence reflected in the world. We remove and release the pain and suffering that has filled our hearts, our world, for eons and fill our hearts, our world with love.

A New Beginning

A new filling
through forgiving
the old world shorn;
a new world born.

A new filling
a new beginning,
no past pain;
freedom now reigns.

A new beginning
through forgiving
the past released;
God's Son at peace.

A place of peace
a place of grace;
the Light of God
fills every space.

The Love of God
fills every place;
the Love of God
in every face.

Easter

Through the tunnel,
into the light
the false world vanishes,
no more in sight.

Met by friends
in Heaven above,
no more amends,
just those that we love.

We now know Heaven,
no longer apart;
We now know Heaven,
deep in our heart.

We have risen,
the Christ is reborn;
A holy place given—
A new day now dawns.

The Gift of Aloha

I had a dream about spraying. I was renting a condominium in Hawaii and was there when someone was spraying—spraying to keep mice at bay. I felt the fumes in my lungs. I wished I had come to Hawaii another time. I needed to go outside, to be by the ocean, to breathe fresh clean air, to breathe. Then I awoke.

I awoke to the clean air of my home. I awoke and realized that humanity has been spraying the toxic fumes of the ego for eons, fumes of judgment, hatred, and attack. We have separated ourselves from each other, from our environment, from God.

We have been dreaming. As we awaken, we will know the truth; we are one with all creation, we are one with God. In truth, we are holy, we are loving, we are kind. In truth, we are innocent.

Spraying appears to offer comfort, safety. The toxic fumes of the ego offer no salvation, no comfort, only its appearance; the fumes of death offer no life.

Now is the time for the Great Awakening. Now is the time to breathe the clean air of our innocence. Now is the time to breathe. Now is the time to live aloha, to live with the Breath of God.

This is our salvation; this is our life. This is the clean air of our Creator.

It is time to breathe, to know the clean air of innocence in each other and deep within our hearts. It is time to be by the ocean, to be in Living Water, to bring aloha to the world.

Aloha

Holy Ground
All around,
We stand
On sacred land.

On Holy Soil
we are God's Seed.
On Holy Soil
There are no weeds.

We breathe aloha
from God's Holy Land.
We live aloha
where we now stand.

We are God's Holy Seed.
In His Son, there are no weeds.

A Holy Seed
born in God's Womb,
a Holy Flower
will now bloom.

We are aloha,
from God's Loving Hands
we bring aloha
to the Holy Land.

A Direct Flight Home

Man has been on a long, arduous journey to his final destination—home.

For eons, man has relied on the slow process of evolution, growing, healing over many lifetimes. The situation in the world has worsened to such a degree that a new plan is unfolding; a celestial speedup to bring God's Son home. Helen Schucman, the scribe of *A Course in Miracles,* wrote about this and her part in it in her autobiography:

All the apparent sins we believe we have committed are just that—they are apparent—they are not real. We heal our souls by awakening to the truth of our Essence; we are holy—the Holy Christ Presence lies deep in our hearts; we are God's Holy Son.

We were created as love, by a Loving God. All our apparent sins exist only in dreams. All that is real is God's Love.

We remember our innocence through forgiveness—seeing our innocence reflected everywhere, in everyone for in truth, it is everywhere, in everyone.

God, our Creator, creates only love. Nothing outside His Creation, His Love is real. We are God's Creation—His Love expressed, extended.

Now is the time for forgiveness. Now is the time for the Great Awakening. We have been taking a long, arduous journey on foot and in covered wagons for eons. Now is the time for a direct flight home.

His River Flows

Trying, trying
to hear God's Word
His Voice so dim
when mine is heard.

All the effort,
so hard I try,
I just sit
and start to cry.

I hear the world,
I feel the pain,
then I listen
and hear the spring rain.

Tears of joy
now touch my face;
I feel His Presence,
I know His Grace.

In the ordinary,
in the mundane,
Now God's Voice
is made so plain.

Like a river,
His Word does flow;
The Holy Giver,
His Presence now shows.

Now I listen
Now I see
Now I rest
content to be.

Like the lilies,
No toil or spin,
His Holy Presence
Where it always has been.

Freedom

Peace given
with God's Hand,
Love received
through God's holy plan.

His holy plan,
His Son now free;
God's Son now knows
His sanity.

The insane voice,
the ego's loud call
will now have a gentle fall.

Falling into the abyss,
falling into nothingness.

God's answer
some form of peace.
God's answer
our sweet release.

We Are God's Message

I awoke early this morning, stretched, and prayed. My mind felt blank. I felt the shock of living in a world with a pandemic, of living in the world. I felt the shock of the separation from our Source that has been reflected in this world for eons, for lifetimes. I felt it deep in my marrow, deep in my heart, deep in my soul.

I asked God to give me His Words. I asked the help of Jesus Christ. I asked His Direction, His Way.

I heard His Voice, "We are God's Message." We have a holy purpose given us by our Creator. We bring love, grace, and kindness to the world.

His Message is deep in our hearts, our souls. It is who we are; it is the message of love.

God's Message has been dormant for eons—for lifetimes—hidden in dreams, in a dream of being separate from our Source.

It is not the truth. In truth we are holy; in truth we are one. We are in this world but not of it.

God's Message is deep in our hearts, our souls. We have a holy purpose; to awaken, to remember, to love.

We bring Heaven's Light to the world. We are God's Message; we are the messengers of love.

Awakening

The angry gods
we must appease,
many moods
so hard to please.

The angry gods,
the ego's dream,
with no love
the ego's scheme.

The world made real,
an unreal place,
so surreal
without grace.

To please a boss,
husband, or wife
we feel the loss.
We feel the strife.

Teenage girls
hear the world's call,
They walk in fear
to the shopping mall.

In the world
we work, we strive,
Trying hard
just to survive.

With every battle,
With every thorn,
We feel tired,
We feel worn.

We ask God's help,
To Him we pray
We ask His help,
A better way.

We ask for love.
We ask for peace.
We ask for help
to give release.

Our Loving Source
answers our prayer.
Our Loving Source
is always there.

The world we made
is but a dream,
It is unreal,
the ego's scheme.

We have awakened
from a nightmare,
no longer shaken,
no longer there.

Our Loving Source,
our lives He does bless.
In His care
we find our rest.

We have come home;
God's holy place,
place of love
Amazing Grace.

A Separate Cove

In a separate cove
there is no love,
no sweet refrain
just the world's pain.

The pain alone
is all that's seen,
in a world
where no light gleams.

His absence felt,
a deep blow dealt
all feels lost
when the ego's boss.

We can awaken
and know God's Light.
His Holy Presence
undoes our fright.

God's Holy Son,
no more afraid.
God always gives
a passing grade.

In God's Kingdom
there is no fright;
In God's Kingdom
just sweet sunlight.

Graduation

In the Silence,
in the dawn,
Our souls have come
to be reborn.

Reborn as holy,
reborn as love;
God's Holy Son
reborn as one.

No more losses we need to recoup;
we are one with our soul group.

Our holy community
is not small.
Our holy community
includes us all.

Is Jesus in Heaven?
Does He go to school?
Or is He free
of the ego's harsh rule?

Jesus takes no classes,
no Heavenly school;
His Holy Christ Presence
now shall rule.

Forgiveness shines its holy light,
all revealed with new insight.

We have awakened,
we now can see.
It is enough
now just to be.

We have awakened,
we are at home.
We are with God,
no more alone.

For God's Holy Son,
no more earthly class;
through Heaven's Gate
God gives His pass.

No more to toil,
no more to spin.
God's Holy Kingdom
where it always has been.

In God's Hands

In God's Hands,
He shows the way.
In His Heart
we've come to stay.

As it was
before the fall;
as it was,
we've heard His Call.

Restoration
now at hand,
all restored
through His holy plan.

The past undone,
the past released.
His Kingdom comes;
We know God's peace.

Stillness

It's early morning. I had just awoken. I brushed my teeth, prayed, sat. I felt tears of joy. I felt His Guidance to write.

I did not know what I would be writing but I had faith. I trusted Him. I would be given His Message. I would be given His Words.

I still didn't know what I would write as I began this sentence. Then I heard the words, "Be Still."

Stillness is our salvation. Stillness brings us home, for in stillness we are home. Stillness is sacred, holy. In stillness, we have our rest.

We rest in God. When we are still, we carry His Presence with us. In truth, it is always here.

The world feels devoid of stillness, of holiness. Yet we can shine His Holy Light even here. Stillness is our essence, our ocean of being, our home.

We are at home in our Creator. When we are still, we awaken, we know—we know the Presence of God.

In Him we live, move, and have our being. In Him we find our rest, our salvation. In Him we are home.

On Eagles' Wings

On eagles' wings
we touch the sky.
On eagles' wings
now we fly.

No longer trying,
no effort made;
The world below
now does fade.

Fading now the world below,
now the feel of Heaven's glow.
Heaven's glow, all around,
We fly free of earthly sounds.

Gone is the earthly din,
God's Son born without sin.
Born innocent, filled with grace.
Born in a holy space.

Free from prison,
from the earth,
The Christ arisen;
our rebirth.

God's Treasure,
no more to hide.
God's Treasure,
deep inside.

Deep inside our very core.
On eagles' wings, now we soar.

The Dam Released

The dam released,
the water flows.
No longer hidden,
the Light now shows.

Living Water
from the Source.
Living Water,
Our Vast Resource.

Our Vast Resource,
our deep well;
God's Holy Son
freed from hell.

No more suffering.
No pain to hold.
The Glory of God,
now does unfold.

His Living Water,
His Presence clear,
God's Living Water;
His Presence here.

The Way, the Truth, and the Life

Yesterday morning, I wrote an essay entitled *The Way, the Truth, and the Life.* I wrote my words. I did not hear God's. The words felt empty, hollow; they were not His.

I asked for Help: help from Jesus Christ, from the Holy Spirit, from God.

"Jesus, please help me." I felt the release. A space was opening, opening to receive His Message, His Voice, His Love.

God is always here. His Spirit always available. Like static on a radio, my mind was filled with noise. Even though He was always there, I could not hear Him nor feel His Presence.

I prayed. I listened. I let go. I heard. I felt the Silence. I felt His Presence; my soul renewed, restored.

In our world, on the Earth, man has been busy living in the noise, the hustle and bustle of ordinary life. We have not opened the space for the Silence; we have not opened the space for God.

The busyness, the hustle and bustle, has masked our deep pain of trying to live apart from our Source.

Now is the time to awaken. Now is the time to come home. In truth, we are never apart from our Creator, for we are a part of His Kingdom; we are one with all creation.

When we are still, we know the truth. We know His Holy Presence. We know the holiness of all creation, of all life. We know our unity; we know we are one with God.

Our One Friend

Our One Friend
always there;
Like an oak
He will us bear.

He shares the load,
His Strength at hand,
He carries us
to the Promised Land.

He does not judge.
He holds our hand.
He holds no grudge
with Him we stand.

His Love,
Our Rock;
He holds us all
In His Arms
we cannot fall.

We know love.
In Christ we rest.
We live in God,
His Holiness.

Seeds of Joy

Seeds of joy
touch my face.
Love has bloomed;
Amazing Grace.

Amazing Grace,
God's Grace shows
tears of joy;
the river flows.

With forgiveness
I now rest.
I now have
such happiness.

Deep joy, in my soul.
God's Love fills my bowl.

Like a flower,
like a tree,
we can flower;
we can be.

We can rest in
a holy place.
We can rest,
Amazing Grace.

He Directs My Steps

He directs my steps,
I cannot fall.
He always sees me
through it all.

Through it all,
a clear marked trail
on His path,
I cannot fail.

Through the dark,
through the maze,
with His clear eyes
there is no haze.

There is no haze,
the trail so bright.
He guides us home with
His Holy Light.

The Path

He guides my day,
His holy trail,
He shows the way;
I cannot fail.

Through His Presence
He guides us all.
With His Love
We cannot fall.

On His Shoulders
we now stand.
He clears the boulders
from the land.

God's Direction,
we heed His Call.
God's Perfection
is in us all.

Love Makes No Comparison

I was feeling tired and not very spiritual. I did not feel inspired to write. No words came. Grievances did. Then I saw what matters, what is truly of value. All that matters, all that is valuable, is the Holy Christ Presence that is in each of us; all that is valuable is God, His Creation.

I felt a new energy, a new vitality, a new life.

I thought about my friend Marjorie Tyler. Margie, along with Jo and Meera, has scribed several volumes of the *One With God* books. I was comparing the book I'm writing with her books. Then I saw the obvious; the truth. I was not called to scribe the *One With God* books. I was called to write *Love Created Us; Living a Life That's Holy.*

Each of us has a calling, a special part in God's plan for salvation. Our life, our calling is priceless; it is holy. It is from God. Heaven would be incomplete without any part of His Creation.

As the Prodigal Son discovered, he was his father's treasure. We are God's Treasure.

A drum is not a trumpet, is not a violin, is not a piano. All of us are called to be God's instruments.

We each have a part in God's plan for salvation. He is the Maestro, the Conductor. He will give us direction. He will lead us home.

A Holy Birth

He gives the words.
He gives His Thought.
He shines His Light.
What has God wrought?

He sows the seed.
He plants His Lawn.
The seed does sprout
a new soul born.

Conceived in love,
Conceived in grace,
from God above,
a holy place.

A place of birth,
a place of grace.
He knows his worth;
Joy lights his face.

A new day dawns
with love conceived;
a child is born,
the love received.

Looking Inside

Where do I look?
What do I see?
Do I feel His Presence
looking back at me?

On the computer,
on the web,
or in my heart
is His Presence felt?

The web of Earth
now released,
my soul's rebirth;
my soul at peace.

His Holy Presence,
God does not hide.
It's easy to find
when you look inside.

Resting

We can rest,
we can be.
In His Presence
we are free.

His Gifts

A new beginning; His plan alone brings freedom. Listen to God. Hear His Voice. He is the Way, the Truth, and the Life. He gives His gifts, His Love. He brings us home.

We rest in God. He alone gives solace. Come to Me and I will give you rest.

Rest for the weary. A lonely journey ends. Solace, grace, happiness, joy, peace: these are God's gifts for His Son.

The Holy Guest

I feel tired,
I want to rest;
don't feel inspired
by the Holy Guest.

I sit, I wait;
the load is here.
I feel blank,
the weight I bear.

I give my pen
to the Holy Guest;
all the words
in Him I rest.

I rest in God,
the light now comes;
with His Love,
I see the sun.

His Light now shines–
awake, alert–
I feel the joy,
a new rebirth.

The world's tasks,
no need to do;
In Him I rest.
He pulls me through.

He pulls me through
to my one goal;
with His Love
He heals my soul.

My soul in God,
in Him I rest.
I am one
with the Holy Guest.

Opening

There's more to write.
There's more to say.
God gives His Voice;
He shows the way.

He leads us gently
through the maze.
A clear path
beyond the haze.

A new day dawning,
God's Gift revealed.
The Door to Heaven
now unsealed.

The Door now open,
I can now see
His Holy Vision,
restored to me.

The Holy Driver

The space between the notes is essential to a beautiful melody, a great symphony. A continual sound would not be music; it would just be noise.

Man has been making a continual sound, a continual noise, for eons. It is the sound of the ego, the ego's senseless shrieks.

Now is the time for God to write a beautiful symphony. Now is the time to receive God's beautiful Symphony. Now is the time to play our part in God's Symphony. God writes the symphony. His Presence rights our life.

Mankind has been asleep to the Celestial Melody, the beautiful music of God's Life, of His Creation. Humanity has felt guilty for taking time, taking space, to be with God.

I direct your steps. You have given your life to God, to Jesus, to Me, the Holy Spirit.

I am very efficient. As you let Me do the driving, you will find I am an excellent driver. I drive safely, efficiently, effortlessly; I drive with Love.

Man has tried to drive his own car for eons, for lifetimes. What has it wrought but pain? What has it wrought but heartache? What has it wrought but suffering?

It is time for a new way, a new driver. Time for Me to do the driving. Time to enjoy the ride, to know the ease, grace, happiness, and peace of God. I will bring you home.

Sitting

I sit with God,
in Him I rest.
I sit and feel
the Grand Bequest.

No plans to make
no row to hoe.
I sit, I wait;
my soul does show.

The Christ in me,
all that is real;
the Christ in me,
no more concealed.

A simple day,
no other plans.
He is the Way,
I now understand.

The sunlight shines,
the grass so green.
I feel His Love,
His Presence seen.

No plans to make;
He runs the show.
I sit, I rest;
with God I go.

Letting Go

Letting go
of my plans
of having my feet
on shifting sands.

In His Heart,
His Love abounds.
Now I stand
on solid ground.

On His lawn,
I can now rest.
In His Presence
I feel so blessed.

I can rest
by His lake.
In His Living Water
does my soul wake.

I wake in God.
I now let go.
It is not hard;
the river flows.

The river flows
gently downstream.
I wake in God.
No more to dream.

God's Melody

I await the call,
God's Word to hear.
He tells us all;
His message clear.

I write the words
He gives to me.
His message heard,
my soul is free.

I sit, I wait—
no words do flow—
in Holy Silence
His Presence shows.

With quiet sounds,
God sings to me.
His song so sweet;
God's Melody.

The Return Home

I feel blank, quiet, ready, alert. I see the budding green leaves on the trees in front of my apartment.

Signs of spring are everywhere. New life. New blossoms. Today, I walked up the hill behind my apartment. I saw the many-colored beautiful windflowers; the renewal of spring.

I feel the tears; the tears of greeting a long-lost friend. I feel empty yet filled with joy, freshness, rebirth.

We have lived through long winters on the Earth; long winters, hot summers. It is time for renewal, for spring.

We are returning home, home to God's Kingdom; the deep place of love, of joy, of peace in our hearts. In truth, we have never left His Kingdom. The long winters and hot summers were only in our dreams.

This is the time to awaken, to know the beauty of spring in every heart.

The beauty of the wildflowers, of the new leaves, reflect the beauty in everyone. This Holy Christ Presence has been dormant. Now is the time to awaken, to blossom. Now is the time of the Great Awakening.

Springtime is now here. We are coming home.

His Love Revealed

He plans our day,
He shows the way.
He gives us life.
There is no strife.

The way of peace—
Our life in God—
our struggles cease.
It is not hard.

We pause to rest—
a flowering tree—
we are so blessed,
we can just be.

Heaven's Gate,
no more concealed.
No more to wait,
His Love revealed.

His Heavenly Music

His Heavenly Music
in the trees,
on the land,
on the seas.

In each flower,
in every bird,
His holy music
now is heard.

In each other,
in every heart,
God's sweet notes
have their part.

We can see
with His Sight.
We can live
in His Light.

The Shepherd's flute
now sounds clear,
in every heart
we hold dear.

Infinity

Infinity's Presence
not the norm.
Infinity's Presence
beyond form.

The depth of God
all around,
His Holy Music
makes no sound.

In Silence born,
in Love conceived;
the old world shorn,
the new received.

A holy place
in every heart;
beyond time and space,
we're not apart.

We are a part
of the whole,
His Holy Presence
fills every soul.

His Gentle Harvest

He plants the grain,
the seed is sown;
with gentle rain,
His Harvest grown.

Grown in love
on hallowed ground,
His Gentle Presence
all around.

We live in Him,
He soothes our souls.
His Gentle Presence
fills our bowls.

His Loving Touch,
His Kind Hand;
His Loving Presence
heals the land.

He heals the land.
He fills our bowl;
with His Love,
we are now whole.

All in Order

This afternoon, I was writing a table of contents for my book. I did not know in what order to have the poems and writings. I decided, for the most part, to keep them in the order I received them.

Afterwards, I felt hungry. I felt tired, not inspired to write. I sat with God, with the Holy Spirit, and heard His Words, "All in order."

I let go. I trusted the Still Small Voice of God. Even when life appears chaotic, there is order—God's. There is grace, there is beauty; even in what appears mundane.

There is order in writing a table of contents for a book. There is the Presence of God everywhere—in everything. There is a holy plan for our lives. He guides our steps. He shows the way for He is the Way, the Truth, and the Life.

We can listen to the Still Small Voice of God and live a life that's kind, loving, holy. There is a deep place of peace, of grace, of love that is in the world but not of it; it is Our Essence, it is Our Holy Christ Presence.

We are God's instruments of salvation. We have a holy purpose; to bring His Love to the world.

His Holy Plan

All in order
with God's Hand.
All in order
God's holy plan.

A plan to wake,
a plan to live;
His holy plan,
to us God gives.

Salvation here,
now at hand;
He gives to us
His holy plan.

With God's Love
we understand,
we have God's peace;
His holy plan.

A Simple Day

A simple day—
a simple life—
God shows the way,
there is no strife.

The effort made
to hear His Voice.
His plan relayed;
we can rejoice.

His Guidance sure,
His Gift received;
holy and pure,
we sit relieved.

We rest in Him,
our Vast Resource;
we know His Love—
our Loving Source.

God's Beautiful Words

God's Beautiful Words;
I play the notes,
I sing the songs
that He wrote.

I write the words
He gives to me.
All that I've heard,
I share with thee.

In the sky,
on the land,
is His Presence—
is His Hand.

In our souls,
deep inside,
His Holy Presence
does reside.

We are His Words,
His Holy Seed.
His Message heard;
His Voice received.

In Kindness Born

In Kindness, born.
In Love, conceived.
A new day dawns,
the love received.

A new world born
without end.
We go with
Our Holy Friend.

A new beginning,
God's Holy Way.
We are home—
Home to stay.

The senseless journey,
no more made.
His Holy Child,
no more afraid.

In His Arms
we now rest,
with His Love
we are blessed.

Eternity
now at hand.
Home at last;
God's Holy Land.

Where Are We Investing?

His Presence, all that matters.
His Presence, all that's real.
The world of illusions,
does His Presence conceal.

Where are we investing?
Is it in God alone?
Are we taking detours,
or following the direct route home?

Where are we living?
Where are we home?
With all the world's glitter,
we feel so alone.

We are always in His Presence,
always in His care.
He is always with us.
He is always there.

We can awaken
from the glitter and the gold;
We can remember.
His Love does us enfold.

All in God's Hands

In God's Hands,
He lifts us up,
with His Love
He fills our cup.

He shows the way,
He guides us all,
with His Love
we cannot fall.

His blessings here.
His holy place.
He holds us dear,
all pain erased.

We have come home,
all in God's Hands.
All is restored;
His holy plan.

Buried Treasure

Buried Treasure
so long denied,
so long hidden,
so long disguised.

Under the covers,
under the earth;
God's Holy Son
now knows His worth.

God's Loving Presence,
the truth now seen.
The Son awakens
no more to dream.

We are God's Treasure.
His Gift revealed
Our Holy Light;
no more concealed.

We are God's Treasure,
His Gift Divine.
Our Holy Light,
so brightly shines.

Our Holy Essence

There was a silent movie called Wings made in 1927. There were two American aviators in the film. They were friends. One was shot down behind German lines. He was able to get a German plane and fly it. The other American aviator saw the German plane and started shooting. He did not know that the pilot was his friend.

The American aviator saw the package; a German plane. He did not see his friend. All of us have different packaging. All of us have the same Holy Essence.

Everyone wants to be valued, to be seen, to be known, to be loved. Our hearts cry for acceptance, kindness, love.

There are signs saying Black Lives Matter. This is true; Black lives do matter. I have thought, why does it matter whether someone is Black, White, Asian, Hispanic, male, or female when Our Holy Essence is the same inside?

The packaging may be different. Like the American aviator, we may not see that the packaging conceals the presence of a friend.

Now is the time to look inside—inside the package—and know the truth: we are the same inside, we are one with each other, we are one with God.

Our Holiness Reclaimed

Beyond the sin,
beyond the stain,
beyond the ego's
sad refrain.

Beyond the world,
beyond the guilt,
beyond the ego's
patchwork quilt.

God's Child unsoiled,
God's Child unstained,
in innocence born—
our holiness reclaimed.

Born in Love,
conceived in Grace;
we are from
God's holy place.

The world released,
the dream undone,
in God we rest;
we have come home.

His Holy Way

I sit, I listen.
I wait, I hear.
The Voice of God
is so clear.

His Holy Presence
now I feel.
God's Holy Presence
all that's real.

I wait in silence.
A quiet day
with His Love,
He shows the way.

God's direction,
His holy way;
deep inside us,
His Love does stay.

The Weaver

He weaves His thread.
He sews His cloth.
A new life
He does bring forth.

He plants His Seeds
on His Grounds;
a gentle crop,
new life abounds.

Beautiful flowers
now in bloom;
beautiful cloth
from God's Loom.

His music plays
a sweet sound.
God's angels
all around.

All around
the earth and sky,
with His Love,
we can fly.

We fly home
to His Land.
He lifts us up.
He holds our hand.

A Soft Landing

A soft landing
for us all.
We come home,
we hear His Call.

A gentle path,
we rejoice.
A gentle journey,
we hear His Voice.

We rest
on soft sand.
We receive
God's holy plan.

On God's Blanket,
His Child does sleep,
in His Arms
no more to weep.

We now rest
in God's Embrace.
We are home;
a holy place.

A Quiet Place

A quiet place
with God I rest;
a quiet place,
I feel so blessed.

All the load
the burdens borne;
all the load
now is shorn.

I let go
in my chair.
Here I sit,
no load to bear.

My innocence
restored to me.
I can sit.
I can be.

A new beginning,
a new day,
a new life;
God's Holy Way.

Homecoming

We release the world
its false joy,
an empty place;
the ego's toy.

No more glitter,
no more gold.
A new life
does unfold.

No excitement,
no fast race.
A peaceful journey
filled with grace.

God's Love
in every step.
His Holy Presence,
His Promise kept.

We come home;
His Kingdom here
in our hearts,
His Love so clear.

Where Are We Shopping?

Where are we shopping?
What will we buy?
In whose store
do we want to try?

Bells and whistles
are in one store,
filled with glitter—
glitter galore.

The emptiness hidden,
the glitter is seen;
the emptiness hidden
by a senseless dream.

A dream of suffering—
the ego's bequest—
a dream of pain,
a dream of death.

We can awaken
and try a new store
filled with love,
which offers us more.

A holy place,
what God has in store,
for His Holy Son
as we walk through His Door.

To Plan a Day

To plan a life,
to plan a day.
Who makes the plans?
Who shows the way?

His Guidance sure,
simple and clean,
with Love so pure,
beyond the dream.

His Holy Voice,
He gives His Words
we make the choice,
His Message heard.

We now let go,
our plans released.
He runs the show,
we have God's peace.

With God I Go

With God I go,
a gentle walk;
in His flow,
a quiet talk.

Filled with love,
filled with light,
an easy path;
there is no strife.

I come home.
I come to rest,
a quiet place
where I am blessed.

I now let go.
I rest, I breathe.
His place of peace,
I now receive.

On His Shoulders

On His Shoulders
we now stand;
solid rock,
not shifting sands.

He takes our hand.
He lifts us high,
with His Love
we now do fly.

Now secure
in God's Embrace,
all past pain
He does erase.

We come home
no more to stray;
here we rest,
here we stay.

A Simple Life

A simple life,
a holy way,
a life of joy,
a brand-new day.

We have our birth
in God alone;
in Him, we live—
our holy home.

A place of peace,
a place of love;
our holy home,
Heaven above.

Above the world,
above the fray;
a place of love
for us to stay.

We rest in God,
a holy place
filled with love.
Amazing Grace.

A New Day Dawns

A new day dawns;
the Light now shines
the Light of God,
the Light Divine.

We see the sun.
We see the sky.
We are God's Son,
we fly so high.

Heaven bound,
no earthly days;
one with God,
no earthly ways.

The joy, the grace;
His Love Divine.
A holy place,
the sun does shine.

Tears of joy;
we know His Grace.
Now at home,
a holy place.

The joy, the grace;
His Light now shines,
a holy place,
for His Son Divine.

Home

Sit with Him.
His Voice now heard;
His Holy Presence
beyond words.

An opening
His holy way
Our life in God
with Him we stay.

We have our rest.
We have God's peace;
a quiet place
with grace and ease.

We walk with Him
with open hearts.
One with God,
the dream departs.

The Love of God
deep in our hearts;
we are home,
no more apart.

His holy place,
His Loving Words,
a quiet place,
His Message heard.

With deep gratitude to
Marjorie Tyler, Sharon Lund, Sara Niccolls,
Katie Palm, Bill Van Nimwegen, Helfried Zrzavy,
Jennifer Pryor, Joann Sjolander, and Margaret Ballonoff.

From the Holy Spirit
A New Page

I have directed your life from the beginning. All planned. Homecoming – coming home to God. Your feeling of separation from your biological family mirrored your feeling of separation from God. Your relationship with your grandmother was holy, loving, and kind, and reflected God's Love.

I had you meet Margie on your favorite beach in 2003. You have a holy relationship built on the Solid Rock of kindness and love, the Firm Foundation of God.

Her messages from Me awakened your heart to My Holy Presence.

The Holy Christ Presence is in everyone, everywhere. This is the time for the Great Awakening of humanity, to remember our unity with each other and with God.

www.ingramcontent.com/pod-product-compliance
Lightning Source LLC
LaVergne TN
LVHW020632100826
845148LV00012B/2153

9781735693262